T0067554

As I Discover
My Child

As I Discover My Child

PRITI SARAOGI

PARTRIDGE
A Penguin Random House Company

Copyright © 2014 by Priti Saraogi.

ISBN:	Hardcover	978-1-4828-1650-1
	Softcover	978-1-4828-1649-5
	Ebook	978-1-4828-1648-8

All rights reserved. No part of this book may be used or reproduced by any means, graphic, electronic, or mechanical, including photocopying, recording, taping or by any information storage retrieval system without the written permission of the publisher except in the case of brief quotations embodied in critical articles and reviews.

Because of the dynamic nature of the Internet, any web addresses or links contained in this book may have changed since publication and may no longer be valid. The views expressed in this work are solely those of the author and do not necessarily reflect the views of the publisher, and the publisher hereby disclaims any responsibility for them.

To order additional copies of this book, contact
Partridge India
000 800 10062 62
www.partridgepublishing.com/india
orders.india@partridgepublishing.com

CONTENTS

Priti Saraogi, a Chartered Accountant and a graduate from Shri Ram college of Commerce, takes pleasure in introducing herself as a mother of three little angels—Ananya, Pallavi and Suhaani than anything else. She believes that raising children is a precious blessing showered upon any mother and can be admirably balanced with professional and house responsibilities; if you persuade yourself to cherish it each day and besides being a mentor to her child, you let them be your teachers as well.

When I walked through the path of life

. . . . I desired to be the best scholar

. . . . Subsequently, the best professional

. . . . Then the best daughter

. . . . The best companion

And then came a phase . . . .

When I just wanted to be a Mother

PREFACE

I THINK THAT A WOMAN falls in love twice in her life—once with her companion and then with her motherhood. And I suppose once she is a mother, this role very naturally supersedes the others that she is trying to balance out every day.

This compilation is a collection of my factual experiences with my daughters; Ananya, Pallavi and Suhaani. I started to pen them down; one because I take pleasure in writing. It just makes me cheerful to have expressed my thoughts in words. Second because I did not want to let go the incredible moments my children brought to my life. I began for my selfish interest, just so that I could relive them later in years.

People ask me often, how I manage three children and I only think back in surprise; 'How would life be without even one of them?'. 'INCOMPLETE', that is the only answer I get from within. Yes, that is so truthful and one can only value it once they possess what I do.

Why the name' As I discover my child'? Writing is a way to heal. Through writing I realized I was also sorting out a lot of stress and variances of growing up—a few of mine and a few of my children. I would come to grips with them and their problems far better.

This anthology is an endeavor to bring to light a few things that I learnt on my journey as a mother—some from my offsprings and some from my lapses as a mom. And all of us are kind of aware but we never sit down and consciously comprehend the same. Therefore, I intend to continue with this newly discovered passion so that each day I am advancing to be a delightful mom.

In this diligent effort, besides my three dolls I would like to thank Gagan, my husband, who enthused me to write. And of course, Dr. Vidya Gupta, a renowned Neonatologist, whom I consider as the one who brought my angels to my life and gave me the right direction on the way to raising them—To relish and prize their upbringing.

I Wish To Be A Child Again

MATURE AND RESPONSIBLE
Experienced and composed
At this juncture of my life
I recall and think to force
In the hush-hush of my busy years
I shed the mischief of childhood
They say I grew up
And I say I ceased being beautiful

People tell me
Childhood and age has no connection
Wish I could have faith in them
When I know that it's a sheer delusion.
I realize I can't repossess
Those cozy peaceful years
Where happiness was natural
With epoch it disappeared.
Beauty of trees and sky so blue
Soiling with mud all about
Pleasure in spilling the food

Melody in the birds humming around
With bicycles chasing butterflies
Climbing and tumbling down
Picking flowers and hating nap time,
Playing with blocks and no time bounds

Success comes from snatching a toy from your kin
And life goes tipsy if you don't win
Award means a little hug from Mom
Punishment means despised food from home
Where it's perfectly legal to cry
And you always have your parents to stand by
But to thank for those beautiful years we shy
We don't realize how time will fly

And the carefree life
Is hard to get back
Hope, Joy, truth
When you live only on principles like that
Where achievements have no limits
And failures you never have
Where Joy is laying head on Mom's bosom
And riding on your dad's back

Alas! You grow up to guileless youth
The world brings its dark code to you!
Growing up, aaaah
is a terribly hard thing to do.
As I see my children
One thing I take time to do
Is find solace in their innocence
To experience the same childhood simplicity anew

A star, a flower, a gush of rain,
Often makes me seem a child again
In the hush-hush of my busy years
I shed the mischief of childhood
They say I grew up
And I say I ceased being beautiful.

The Big Question "Will I Be Able To?"

A baby asked God, "They tell me you are sending me to earth tomorrow, but how am I going to live there being so small and helpless?"

"Your angel will be waiting for you and will take care of you."

The child further inquired, "But tell me, here in heaven I don't have to do anything but sing and smile to be happy."

God said, "Your angel will sing for you and will also smile for you. And you will feel your angel's love and be very happy."

"Who will protect me?"

God said, "Your angel will defend you even if it means risking it's life."

the child hurriedly asked, "God, if I am to leave now, please tell me my angel's name."

"You will simply call her, 'Mom.'"

I had read this story when I was just a child and looked upto my mom for what role she had played in my life. Then, I didn't know or probably I didn't realise, that someday I'll be a mom too . . . . I'll be an angel as well and that too to my two cute little girls. Yes, I have Twins—Ananya and Pallavi.

When I came to know I am expecting twins, the big question struck me as well "Will I be able to handle it?" I know I know I have been always passionate about little ones and was quite ardent to have my own. But to know that you'll soon have double the responsibility dawning on you, you certainly tend to become wary of your own abilities.

They are more than a year now. I can recollect every moment I have spent with them. I have a log of every little milestone, their likes, their dislikes and most importantly how different they are from each other. But honestly, amidst all this, I have never felt, not even once, that I can't handle them. Its just an anxiety which I suppose every mother confronts at the outset of motherhood.

Yes, its true that having a child is a revolutionary step in your life. Your schedule is suddenly run by their time table, but think about it, do you really care to do anything else beyond them? Their endless gurgles don't let you concentrate on anything but try sending them to their grandparents for a day, the silence would kill you. Their constant nagging as they eat their lunch gets on to your nerves. But guess what, you'll soon find yourself sitting again and planning for what they'd like to have for dinner. True, they mess around the house and it's a pain to keep it clean. But did a spic n span home ever gave you as much pleasure as their charming actions, when they enjoy spilling your lovely sofa? They bring in a significant change in your relationship with your husband but have you and your husband ever felt so complete before they came into your lives?

Just take sometime off and ask yourself. Everything changes from your wardrobe, your room, your married life to even your vocabulary. But so what, this is not the time you wonder about how it will all be done. This is the time, THE time to live every bit of it because you can get all the time in the world to work, to read, to do every little thing that you have always wanted but you WON'T EVER get their first 2 years back when they do so many things the FIRST TIME—When they say their first word, they first roll over, they dance, they take their first step, their first climb, their first sentence.

Once tiny babies would grow too fast and you really can't do anything to make these moments last. So just stop worrying and start enjoying.

Ask me how proud I felt when I got a call the other day, 'Can I please speak to Pallavi's mom? And it only fills my eyes with tears when I ask my elder one my favourite question "Ani, You love Mumma?" and she nods with such an adorable smile saying YES.

When we try to teach Pallavi to say a few new words, I can't help feeling so elated when she refuses to utter anything except her favourite one—"Mumma". Even I have called out this word more than a thousand times to my mom but I truly didn't know what it means to her until now. Frankly, I don't know if I can be what God has told them but to me they are my Angels, my World.

"When you are a mother, you are never alone in your thoughts"

THE DILEMMA

WORK OR CHILDREN? OR Both? That's a tough one. I am ready to reward anyone who can answer that with ease, with undoubted surety. A question I believe every woman faces it these days. I still do.

People tell me that it's not the amount of time that matters; it's the quality time that you spend with your child. But hello, if I try to spend the day doing just as much as is really important to my children, I don't know where my time flies, forget about quality time.

I want to be a perfect mom, a little close to that at least. Be right there waiting, when they rush out of school just dying to see me . . . . Applaud them on their little achievements . . . . read out stories as they sleep into their sweet dreams . . . ensure an amazing meal . . . . play with them to infinity like a child . . . . and find answers to their ceaseless needless but obvious questions.

But what also concerns me is how I can continue to work. I would like to devote a portion of my time to work as a minimum. Something on the lines what I truly consider one needs to grow on in life. I also want to be a role model to my children of how I proficiently manage both.

I can tell you the decision is quite baffling and thinking about it more, leaves me only more perplexed. The fact is that one does not have optimum energy levels all day long. While, as much as I try to will myself not to feel tired, the truth is, I do get tired. The dilemna grows.

And then, I close my eyes and remember.... I grew more independent because my parents truly were my pillar in my pre-adolescent years. Maybe because they were always there for me, I am so sharp and responsible. It's how they raised me that way—not so much because of anybody else that I came across or any institution that I ever went to—that has influenced my eventual decisions of life.

I guess the decision is made; it's just that you have to have the courage to accept it. Giving time to your child is not a cost you pay for fore-going your career, it's an investment of your time to nurture her life, a life which you decided to give her and she trusted you completely on that. If a mother realises how vital her care is to a young baby 'it may make it easier for her to decide that the extra satisfaction she might receive from an outside job, is not so important after all'

My dear little girls, truly on the brink of facing the big (bad?) world out there, are going to be off to primary by next year. As much as I want to protect them from the cruelties of growing up, I know I can't . . . so my next best choice is to hold their hands and walk them through it as far as I can.

And it only makes me proud of this decision. It's not a compromise.

"I'll always need my children no matter what age I am. My children
have made me laugh . . . made me proud . . . made me cry . . .
hugged me tight . . . seen me fall . . . cheered me up . . . kept me
going strong . . . and driven me crazy at times! But my children
are a promise from god that I will have a friend forever."

My Baby's First Birthday Party

'PLEASE DO COME TO my birthday party. Rishav.'; read the invitation to my daughter which her classmate had sent her. I was pleased to take her out, all jazzed up with the idea that next month, as she turns three, even she can have a bash with her friends.

Honestly, that visit to Rishav's celebration, put an end to my confusion as to how I should plan my darling's upcoming birthday. I decided NOT TO celebrate it, atleast not the way most of us define celebration.

The party was organized at one of the most renowned places with a nice play pen for the little ones, with the widest choice of food for children that they can even think of and the most delicious cake one can ask for. They had huge number of games, grand decoration, back presents and extraordinary invitations.

Everything was delightful but the birthday boy. He was only cranky to see massive number of new faces around and eventually too tired to cut the cake (his most awaited event of the day), waiting for all his loving guests to arrive. Play pen? Did he enjoy it? I don't think he even got time to see it. And talk about the mouth watering delicacies, he was least concerned to even taste them.

I understand all parents are eager to celebrate their child's first birthday. It's as if they wish to announce to the world that it was this day they were endowed upon the honour of being called mom-dad and that their little happiness that was gifted to them exactly a year back has grown so big and adorable. So, they whoop it up; Spend money, time and energy; make it anything but comfortable for the babe-in-arms. What's also bothering is how parents dress them up in sophisticated outfits only to brag how attractive their child can look.

Some argue that it's this way that their child shall learn to socialize and get the exposure to mingle with loads of people. Let me ask you how many of us have had such birthday get-togethers when we were so young? Not many but still we are perfectly comfortable being social. Aren't we?

My point is that such get-togethers for such tiny babies is too early to worry about their exposure to the outside world. They are already coping up with a lot to step into an independent childhood from being a toddler. Interestingly, please recognize that 'Your time' is in fact the ideal gift for your child. Taking him out to a nice playground where you can spend more time together with your undivided attention would make him feel more loved and special than any party which takes away all your mind leaving you drained out, with almost no time for the two of you.

I guess most of us haven't given it a good thought. We sometimes tend to follow the league. Reason it out like I did and on your tot's next birthday, rejoice in an environment where he is happy and cheerful, in clothes, in which he can smile and cut the cake at a time which does not tire or annoy him.

"Your children need your presence more than your presents:"

—Jesse Jackson

DIFFICULT TO BE SIMPLE

M Y SCHOOL TEACHER HAPPENED to teach me a very important lesson of my life. She said that its simple to be important but its more important to be simple. A very unadorned line but left a key impression on my mind.

Unfortunately these days children do not learn such ethics at school. Besides the school lessons, they pick up meaningless standards too. Are teachers to be blamed? No, Not really. It's WE, the parents who are to be reproached.

Just yesterday, I had taken my little sweetie to her first school. Both of us were very keen, more so me because it was a mother—toddler program which I really looked forward to wondering what my baby would learn or how would she respond, this being her first time socializing.

But when I entered, forget about my daughter being flabbergasted in the whole new environment, I was myself a little lost. It seemed less of a classroom but more of a fashion pageant of mother and child. They were all astonishingly dressed, worth appreciating. They spoke in a very sophisticated manner which I would love to imitate. But the only uncertainity that ran across my mind was; is this why am I getting my child to the school? Will it be a learning experience for her or something else?

The only consolation was that we were not a part of it. Suhaani and me were way too simple for the bunch. I loved the way she held my hand not wanting to leave it forever as she felt perturbed reaching out to the whole lot of people. I think what she wore or how she spoke was the last thing on our minds. That's what I call simplicity.

We take offense, judge right or wrong, believe in being up market but ask a child who can be as simple. Simplicity is hard to find these days. All of us were children too at some point of time, just as uncomplicated but time and the big bad world forced us to transform. And very obviously few of us passed on that change to our kids, sometimes too early.

There is no harm being in vogue or adjusting to the new society trends or maturing to acquire the wisdom of right-wrong or good-bad. But its important that we do this with a trouble free and unpretentious attitude like a child does. It's the beauty of being polite, down to earth and compassionate that makes us a good human being and not sophistication alone—a principle we must remind ourselves and preach our children.

I wish I can be like my daughter Pallavi, who right after being scolded for her wrongs, goes around imitating me dramatizing the same dialogues with her sister. I wish I could be as simple not to mind when someone yells at me. The day she gets irritated, I guess I'll understand she has matured; She is heading on to become a grown up like me.

Kids arguing: "I hate you! I won't play with you again." So they played apart. After few minutes, they played again and shared toys. WHY? because for kids, happiness is more important than pride.

My Mommy Bestest

O NE DAY WHEN I came home wet in the rain;

My brother asked: why did you not take the umbrella?

Sis asked: why did you not wait till the rain stopped?

Papa angrily scolded, 'You shall realize after getting cold.'

But my mom, while drying my hair said: stupid rain couldn't it wait till my child came home.

That's Mother.

It brings a little nostalgia in my heart reminding me about all the times my mother made it so nice, comfortable and wonderful. Of course, I must have been quite ungrateful then but I do see how important she was in my life and likewise how inevitable I must be in my children's life.

Have you ever experienced the joy of a superstar fame and eminence? I have come across something very close to that. Thanks to my daughter, Ananya who gives me a celebrity welcome every time I come back home. I don't know how it happens but the moment I ring the doorbell, she just knows it and there it goes. I can hear her scream with elation. That thrill in her voice is honestly quite flattering and brings in all the energy after an ever tiring day to sit down and listen to her stories and play with her to her heart's content.

I think we all understand but sometimes we don't take time to stop and realise that our child loves us the most in fact. Her world begins with us and ends on us. And even though she connects to us instantly at birth, it's entirely different when she learns to express it, by words or by action. And this realization dawned upon me only recently.

Once, my father asked Pallavi to sleep with him for the fact that he really enjoyed playing with her. She agreed to the play-bit certainly but kept insisting that she would come back and sleep with me instead. A disheartened grandpa asked her why, only to get the world's most logical explanation; 'Main mumma ki butterfly hun na (I am Mom's butterfly.)'. What a charming answer? That is how I address her after that—My pretty butterfly—the one who spreads so much happiness in my life. I think I need to thank her forever for making me feel so special.

In just four years of their bringing up, I can share numerous such incidents only if my memory would allow. However, an honest confession is that I have been a little thankless and a little foolish too. In the busy and hectic schedule, I have missed to enjoy these moments. I was so bothered by other works that I didn't find time to value them. But I do appreciate it now. I understand that soon they will grow up and their innocence will wane. I need to catch hold of every moment that I can before they tell me "mom! Can I get my space please?"

When we were on the edge of becoming mothers for the first time, we never realized how important we are going to be for this soon-to-come child. Before long, she shall make you feel that sleeping is pleasurable only when you sleep next to her. Its much more cozy and sound. Going to school is fun but having left you behind is one of the biggest trauma that she is coping up with. Chit chatting is great but narrating the whole day's experience to you and your patient listening is one of the best activities she looks forward to.

All these things just go to make you feel that your child is yelling out to everyone "MY MOMMY IS THE BESTEST". And I feel totally privileged to know that. Wow!

"The best thing in this world is to see my daughters smiling and the next best thing is to know that I am reason behind their smile"

Children Do Not Remember Their Fears

I T HAS BEEN SCIENTIFICALLY proven that children do not remember their fears. But it is practically not true. Thanks to us—yes I mean 'WE' parents. We do not let children forget them. I know it is not correct of me to say so. No parent would ever want their child to go through any pain but I guess we do so only unconsciously.

My purpose of bringing up this thought is to share the fact that it made a huge difference in my child's life once I understood the above.

On my nephew's birthday, I made a very keen observation. When my sister's son, Aditya fell down on the road, all of us quite obviously rushed to pick him up. However, my sister hinted us not to react or help him. Unpredictably, Aditya simply stood up and started to play again as if nothing had happened. After a while I noticed my sis silently ensuring if he had injured himself anywhere. The thing was, she dint want him to cry over it and spoil his mood.

Wasn't that superb? Most of us react very obviously and make our own children sad not recognizing that half the time they don't realize only. To further ice it up, we keep reminding them about the pain even though they have forgotten about it totally. A very trivial observation but impactful results. A child is a pool of energy which is too huge to be distorted by a small injury or fall unless he learns to be conscious of it. So why make him aware of a feeling of distress when it does not bring him any good?

You must be thinking that why I am emphasizing this little thing so much. Essentially because that is how it begins. First with a small injury, then fever, then school fights, then exam fears, then peer pressure and then Life as a whole. We instinctively, in trying to do what we call pampering, make them weak, gloomy and dependent upon us.

When I delivered pre-term children, even I would describe it to eternity the difficult conditions they were born under and I would raise my head with pride saying that they are tough children who have coped up with so many injections and turmoil of the ICU(Intensive Care Unit). Phew! I think I was wrong. I should not have quoted it again and not in front of them at least.

They understand and follow so many things. Be it as petty as a small bruise, don't we inevitably keep asking 'mere bête ko chot kahan lag gayi?'(where did you hurt yourself my baby?) or when they get fever, we keep striking the chord 'Aww!!! My darling baby is down with fever?'. Try to notice that the moment we say so, they start enjoying the attention and begin to sulk again about something they were over and done with.

It is unkind of us to do so. We are only trying to coddle our little one. But now I understand there are better ways to do so. I can hug them without talking about their wound. I can cook their much loved food to just make them feel good. I can spend more time narrating a story to them without mentioning their illness.

As I put this into practice, I realise that they are pretty cheerful unlike us even when they are down with viral. They can still play or jump around. In fact it's the most difficult task to get them to rest. So I have learnt my lesson well but only recently. So who is next to follow?

THINK ABOUT IT

I WOULD LOVE TO SHARE this one. Now a days, whenever I meet my friends or family, a much preferred discussion topic always is that how am I managing to be sane with three little kids around when on the other hand most of them are finding it hard with just one? Honestly, like I already mentioned I would not be complete without even one of them; leave alone feeling hassled. After having raised them for five years, I sense that each contributes a little to make a WHOLE ME.

When my intimates and associates ask me this, I am not sure if they are mocking at my fortunate destiny to have a handful of children or they are envious of my non-complaining look or they are trying to compliment me. I certainly do not have an idea but I definitely never feel the need to explain or respond to their inane query.

But here is one thing I always wanted to say. No matter how difficult it is to raise a child; no matter how barmy it gets, we must not state this remark over and over again, at least not in front of them. Just imagine how we would feel if our parents or friends even faintly stated that in front of us. Our children are too juvenile to understand anything now but soon they will begin to and it might be depressing for them to know so.

Lot of you might argue that you never implied anything seriously. I also know none of us ever mean to tell our child that he or she is unwanted. We happen to say it just like that. That is precisely why I want to talk about it and tell you that its not nice to hear that not even as a joke.

Read this: 'I wonder how exactly do I do it but I guess I really trouble my Mom because I have seen her telling her friends that she is quite relieved when I am off to school for four hours. And even though I look forward to holidays so much, she is always concerned as to what exactly will she keep me busy with. I just don't like it.' These are the words of my daughter's friends.

I was quite upset and realized how such a little thing pinched her. In her formative years, this has a long role to play. It is in fact disheartening to hear such words from your own parents especially in front of anybody else. So, when children grow up demanding their own space and no interference, I think we now know how and where it all started.

There is one more unique thing about the contemporary parenting. A few have postponed the decision to have a second child indefinitely for the sake of convenience. Amid being a qualified professional, proficient house maker and a perfect mother, it does get very difficult. I agree. However, we fail to see its significance. Though fate didnt give me too much time to think on those lines but I am so grateful that I did not.

When I see the three of them playing together and commanding me to stay out of their fun pursuit, I do not feel burdened. I feel happy; Happy to know that my child is attached to her siblings much more than me. It only gives me enormous satisfaction and delight. Chit-chatting, role playing, story-telling, screaming, yelling and then suddenly a bear hug and affection right after a combat as if nothing had ever happened; it all seems like a fantasy world. A world that I, being an only child, thought existed merely in fairy tales.

I cherish to know that this bonding can exist solitarily between them and no matter how much I try, my company cannot be as amusing, dynamic and entertaining as their own sisters. And when they grow up,

I can imagine how well they will take care of each other too. Its touching to see how Suhaani ensures that Ananya does not forget to wear her belt to school; And how Ananya helps to keep Pallavi's pencils in her box so that she is not scolded in school; And how Pallavi ascertains that Suhaani finishes her homework on time. Woah! Did I think, all of that was my job?

So, what I intend to imply is that don't be so self-absorbed. Don't leave out the idea of another offspring simply because you will find it more convenient to complete only one homework than two; Or because it suits you more to feed one and put her to sleep than a set of two.; Or because it is less stressful to cope up with the tantrums of a single child than the double act.

It is a vital choice. Look at it this way that we are depriving our own child from privilege of having a kin and also ourselves from the pleasure of raising a younger child. It's a totally different experience and worth every sweat. As for your space, individuality and fatigue, I have only one thing to say. Even though it is exhausting for me to program their essentials each day, I still feel so pleased and satisfied to see my daughters valuing my efforts so much. I think it's incredible. This makes me feel like an achiever and gives me a re-assurance that no other work in this world can give me this ecstatic joy.

"Family's love and affection is a piece of good fortune"

WISH THIS COULD FOREVER STAY

OUR PRECIOUS LITTLE DAUGHTERS, with sweetness from above
Filled our years with laughter, and lives with lots of love.
Six months old, full of fun; A blink of an eye, you suddenly were one,
In a flash, Seems like time just flies away,
How much I wish this moment could forever stay

A little bit of sunshine, As you laughed with your eyes every day
Your face would cheer us up,
First a smile, then a gurgle to lighten our days
You make us so thrilled with your warm delightful ways
So I captured it all in a camera, and put it in a frame to display
How much I wish this moment could forever stay

You were so much at ease, climbing down the stairs
The toys that you ran for, Is what you really cared
You thoroughly enjoyed, Messing with the clay
I kept a few toys, jotted moments each day
How much I wish this moment could forever stay

As I took you to ice-cream, I taught you to hold it the right way
'Don't let it spill' I would say,
But you loved to lick it in the filthiest way,
So clicked one more picture in my compilation to save
How much I wish this moment could forever stay

How you would hit each other, Push away
I would scold, Expecting that you would obey
I would run on every fight, But all in dismay
It's between sisters you would portray
I only smiled and decided not to disturb your child's play
How much I wish this moment could forever stay

You were growing, Seemed taller every tenth day
Alongside the ever growing sweetness, kept me amazed
Encapsulated your little hand and feet with potter's clay
And Kept them like they would never cease away
How much I wish this moment could forever stay

Your sweet little coo hoo, Was maturing into words' Yeah'!
A phrase, a sentence, a conversation, a story and then an essay
When I asked you any question, you would answer right away
I recorded your voice, to seize the innocence your voice conveyed
How much I wish this moment could forever stay

I tried to teach you school lessons and books in array
Amused me to see how you would run away
Your cute little logics, I would have to give way
So wrote your dialogues, Which when I listen I get swayed
How much I wish this moment could forever stay

Tried to grab hold of your smell, my only regret if I may
I wish I could put it in a bottle, Forever to stay
When you mature, you shall move on and time shall fade away
I will always have these reminiscences as my cells turn grey
As they are my biggest treasures like a memories' bouquet
How much I wish this moment could forever stay.

Pre-school Mom

I RECALL TIME AND AGAIN my father mentioning a citation more often than necessary: Education is not preparation for life; education is life itself. I would wonder then, what is really so remarkable about the quote. But now that I am all set to send my little children to the Big School, I know what it signifies or rather I understand what it meant to him. It meant his life's dream to not only see me educated but also in the most apt way.

When the BIG DAY arrived for my child who has always walked this world holding my finger with her little hands, I must say I was more nervous than her. To realise that my entry would stop at the entrance gate of the school was heart-breaking. How could I trust anybody else for good four hours to take care of my adorable sweetheart? I was amazed though, to see her confidence and excitement as she stepped into the school, her world of first learning—learning of knowledge, of people, of discipline, of life.

There are two incidents which left a marked remembrance on my mind. When Pallavi tumbled down as one of the kids happened to push her in school, I ran to pick her up; "What a careless guy! I am sure it hurt you badly." But no! it touched me to hear my brave little girl say "Mumma, don't' bother. look I am absolutely fine."

I had also freaked out similarly when Ananya's bus turned up almost an hour late from school. And at once, a worried me decided 'I shall drop and pick her personally. However, I changed my mind when I saw how thrilled she was to make friends on her way home and how much she was looking forward to see them the next day. I would have deprived her of that pleasure by being over protective.

Yes that is the word: OVER PROTECTIVE. My entire experience can be summed up in this one word. It was as if my teeny weeny was all ready to mature into a responsible pre-schooler but I was not. In point of fact, I was forgetting how much I would argue with my own parents to let go because I thought I was grown up. To hear a similar thing from your daughter was quite overwhelming.

I am aware that this is just a beginning and I am yet to learn the steps to being a good parent but I want my daughters to know that though it may be a slightly hard for me to let go but I still trust how they shall cope up and deal with challenges—be it in school, work or life.

And even though I am always tied up with one work or the other when they are at home but when they disappear like this together for a four hour span, I genuinely miss them and wait for them to be back; Back to give me the world's most warm hug.

LOVE & NOT PRESSURE GROOMS A CHILD

I HAD ONCE ATTENDED AN interesting lecture wherein they asked us to introduce ourselves with an appropriate adjective before our name. Lets say for example Sweet Suhaani. What brought this to my mind after such a long time? A striking phrase 'Pressurizing Parents' which flashes through my mind very frequently.

'Parents and pressure go hand in hand. Have you ever noticed how much we as parents take load upon ourselves and in turn upon our child to be able to give our best for their supposedly finest lives. No! We don't see it, not at least when we actually do so. We noticed it only when we were children. All of us have gone through it when we were kids but still we find it convenient to forget.

We start this by asking our toddler to sing a poem in front of not one but every single guest that comes to our home. Then follows the most irrelevant explanation of this mean act: It is referred to as an effort to make our child forthcoming and social.

Why? did you and I, who are all settled so amicably in the society with atleast 100 friends on facebook, did we do that willingly when our parents asked us to? No we all hated it. And secondly, why force this upon her when she is so young.

I too was a very shy person and look at me today, I love to be with people. Each one of us have an inherent quality. We may or may not do well academically; may or may not be people-friendly or be good at so many other activities. But that does not give us a reason to pressurize our child consciously or unintentionally.

There is a very famous saying' A child comes through you and not from you.' We must accept that there is a plan for every one on this earth and we must only be guiding agents to what they are and not catalyzing agents trying to force out the best in them.

Amidst all other things like topping in school, Peer pressure, Comparison with siblings, Milestone achievement needs a special mention. The unique thing about it is that this one starts at the age of three months only. Remarkably, this is a new kind of pressure mania we have started at such an age wherein a child does not even know or understand any word except mum.

Does that call for an applaud or does that call for some comprehension and insight?

I have seen parents getting worried about seeing their children spend their early years in doing nothing. What! Is it nothing to be happy? Nothing to skip, play, and run around all day long? Remember, never in his life will he be so busy again and never so relaxed.

I know it's easier said than done. I am myself a parent and its only with time I have realized: To explain or suggest is one thing and to pressurize is another. The best way to put across your kid is to set yourself such targets that she observes and learns from you. It will certainly not help to push her to eternity so that she starts shirking away from you and from her ultimate aim in life.

I think Joyce Maynard, and American author, has put it very aptly 'It's not only children who grow. Parents do too. As much as we watch to see what our children do with their lives, they are watching us to see what we do with ours. I can't tell my children to reach for the sun. All I can do is reach for it, myself.'

"Don't be anxious that your kids never listen to you, be concerned that they are always watching you"

Mumma, Why Did You Scold Me?

T HIS IS MY DAUGHTER'S favourite question these days and to tell you candidly, it's kind of embarrassing when she asks this one in front of anybody and everybody. Then I contemplate two things. One, "Why did I not explain it to her instead of scolding?" Second, "How come such a little girl has the grace to simply inquire me and not react on me for shouting at her?"

It touches me to see that. I determine not to repeat this ever again. However, trust me within not more than two hours I find myself stuck in the same situation and here I am yelling at my little one at one of her mischiefs yet again.

There are times she would insist that I would play with water a little too long; there are times I know if I don't stop her she would hurt herself, but she wouldn't listen; and there are times she picks up wrong habits which she assumes are good and does not care if told otherwise. I don't know what to do and when my sweet negotiations don't work, I get angry.

God! I feel unpleasant. I don't feel alright to see my impatience with such a small child. How come I forget the fact that I despised it so much when my mom would tell me off as a child? What happened to my resolve of becoming a 'never—scolding' mom?

Honestly I have no answer. All I know is that it happens quite often. Children at this age are learning so much and are being exposed to so much that we need to be by their side if not on their head. And being by their side cannot be conditional. It is human to get a bit agitated when they get naughty.

There is no real explanation that I could come up with to my daughter's logical question. What I perceive is that I too shall learn with time. As my child gets bigger with my experience, I shall also mature as a mother with her experience. A marked example that I can share is that the first time my child soddened my clothes, I quickly rushed to take a bath. The second time, I just changed and the third time I didn't care. It's a similar learning experience.

Yes Ofcourse! We must try to be more and more easy going and endeavour to minimize the botheration. That's going to make life simple. But I totally disagree with the modern day philosophy. People mention how children are getting smarter these days and they repel if you scold. You should let your child be. I am not saying guide them to the last level but while they are so tiny, we can take the liberty, not to steer them but to explain them.

I can just say what my dad said. He always believed that it is his duty to at least bring awareness to me. Then it was my call whether to pick that one up or something of my own. I think there was nothing wrong in that. And he has been quite a good dad, in fact an inevitable one.

But what I want to add here is that hope the most prized possession of my life, my daughter understands me forever just like this instant. At all times, she is and will always be most welcome to talk out anything to me and I wish as a grown up, she is never cross with me. I utterly love her and in trying to help her I don't want to lose her affection, not even by an inch. Thus, as I close this note, I make a promise that each day it will only get better and I shall work even harder to become her bestest mom.

"When God made children, he gave me the best ones"

ACCEPTANCE

RECENTLY MY THREE YEAR old young-adult has picked up her favourite word. When I ask her to eat, she replies so spontaneously 'No'; when I tell her to sleep, a Big refusal; when I suggest her to play, I only get a thumbs down; And when I propose that we go to buy her much desired doll, she chooses to buy a teddy instead.

I was reasoning it out the other day as to how she learnt to be so adamant. I would admit that I was the culprit. Was I not the first one to teach her to say no? When she went around crawling the house at eight months, it was me who used to bawl from behind; 'Do not touch that centerpiece.' And over and over again, I kept instructing her with my set of 'No-No—directions'. And here she is, imitating the best of me.

The bad part is that I get quite aggravated to hear that word time and again in the day. But the good part is that she is learning to have a mind of her own. She is learning to exercise her choices. It is just that she is not mature enough to take balanced decisions. And I will have to be more discreet when I handle this kind of behavior.

'It gives me a headache when she cries.' These were my words before I consciously comprehended what is going wrong with my budding daughter. Instead of asking Ananya the reason for her crying, I assumed like always that she was doing so pointlessly. Instinctively, I got enraged only to invite more. The difference was that the crying turned into a howling now. And I was standing at the juncture of an out of control situation with my lost temper and a guilt of scolding alongside.

The thing was that I did not accept her disturbed behavior. I straight away jumped to my righteous conclusion—a conclusion which seemed logical and actually convenient to me. I am not talking about that particular moment only but I had probably either denied or advised or questioned her feelings a lot of times in the day. When she would say I don't feel like going to school; my obvious reactions were:

"No! You must go to school daily or you will not grow up."

"Its for your own interest that going to school is important."

"Why do you have to start the drama of crying before you leave for school, again?"

Not once did I say, "Oh I totally understand if you don't feel like going."

And the day I practiced this surprisingly, within a minute she geared up to go on her own with the sweetest stipulation that she will get her favourite food for lunch when she is back. Woah! I went a step ahead.

Was it that simple? Was it really so uncomplicated? Whatsoever, but I loved it totally. After that I try my best to address her problems and issues by accepting her feelings first before giving my so called valued opinion. This little thing helped me improve my bonding with her and I have come to appreciate her more than before.

Acceptance though not the exhaustive way to deal with your children, it will be an important way. Recognizing or simply agreeing to their feelings before denying them, even if they are incorrect, is of great consequence in making them feel secure.

We should hear them out or let them be before we advise them too soon. Our timing should be appropriate. Like we understand that when a person is drowning, it's not the right time to give swimming lessons. You can explain it slightly later and in a lighter tone. She will be all ears to you then, I promise.

"Children in a family are like flowers in a bouquet: there's always one determined to face in an opposite direction from the way the arranger desires.

—*Marcelene Cox*

WHAT I LEARNT FROM MY CHILD?

As I DECIDED TO teach you the way of life,
It amazed me instead, your innocence would teach me how to enjoy . . .
I would be concerned
For your life and education
Through your untroubled ways of growing up,
You would teach me pleasure lies not in rewards but to try
It amazed me, Your innocence would teach me how to enjoy

I would Get tired
Unable to accomplish all my aims
You would teach me never—ending energy.
Through your infinite chase to snatch a toy
It amazed me, Your innocence would teach me how to enjoy

I would be outraged
At my own imperfection
Through the chuckle that you gave after spilling
You would teach me how to laugh at it even when annoyed
It amazed me, Your innocence would teach me how to enjoy

I would Cry
When anything messed up
Through your warm hug
You would teach me friendships brings joy
It amazed me, Your innocence would show me how to enjoy

I would worry
About being able to take care of you
Through your giggle when you fell from stairs
You would teach me to be carefree, oh boy
It amazed me, Your innocence would show me how to enjoy

I would be anxious
To be successful
Through your smile on finding a small bead
You would teach me genuine victory, ahoy!
It amazed me, Your innocence would show me how to enjoy

I would sulk
When things went wrong
You would teach me never to give up
Incessant efforts for a puzzle you would deploy
It amazed me, Your innocence would show me how to enjoy

I would be hurt
Because I had a sense of self
Through your simplicity to let off your fights
You would teach me 'Please forgive, do not destroy'
It amazed me, Your innocence would show me how to enjoy

I would be finicky
About being organised
Through your grin in the worst of chaos
You would teach me how to unwind and ploy
It amazed me, Your innocence would show me how to enjoy

I would be meticulous
How to speak soberly and sensibly,
Through your screaming everytime you won a game
You would teach me how to have fun and not be coy
It amazed me, Your innocence would show me how to enjoy

I would preach
How to be thoughtful for your loved ones
Through your unparalleled affection for me
You would teach me love and joy
It amazed me, Your innocence would show me how to enjoy.

ENGLISH: OUR NEW MOTHER TONGUE?

BEFORE I SAY ANYTHING further, What do you call 'Mobile' in Hindi? To be honest, even I don't know.

The Title of this write up may sound a bit offending to some, but I believe it's becoming a fact for a large segment of our society. Tell me how many of us say 'Namaste' instead of 'Hi' when we meet our friends or loved ones?

What has forced me to write this, is not one instance but a thousands of them which I have observed since childhood and felt ashamed to know that being Indians, we have started giving a lot more credence to a language (English) other than our own mother tongue.

Forget about others, I am myself trying to teach my two-year old child (who loves to speak Hindi) to start conversing in English. This is out of desperation coz she was not really following what half the world around her was speaking about. On being asked 'what's your name?', my daughter would smile and look at me with a mystifying expression as if 'Mom! What exactly does that mean?' And though she is trying hard to learn her second language, English but I know if someone still asks her "How are you?" her spontaneous answer always is 'Main thik hoon." And then she corrects herself to say "I am fine"

Actually despite everyone's repeated advice, I consciously taught her Hindi first. I had always thought my child must speak her first word or sentence in her mother tongue. And yes, like a brilliant girl as she is, she picked up this language beautifully. But then came the schools and our educational systems and the trouble started.

Unfortunately, English has taken a superior place in our vocabulary and more significantly in our minds. I remember my parents being so worried during my childhood that I did not speak fluent English and that they felt was a serious glitch. Did THEY feel it or the whole gang of relatives made them feel it. I have no clue.

I still can't get over how a salesman spoke so disrespectfully to my mom only because she was trying to explain him what she required in Hindi. When I noticed that, only to teach him a lesson for his impudence, I had to use the right device—THE ENGLISH LANGUAGE. I am sorry to say but it worked. He apologized.

I really respect people by their character and content of they say. The dialect does not matter. Language as dictionary defines it is 'Communication of thoughts and feelings through a system of arbitrary signals, such as voice sounds, gestures, or written symbols.' And as long as one makes himself understood it serves the purpose.

People would argue that I am trying to criticize the global language. I am not. Let's put it this way, had I been against this amazing language, I would not be writing this up in English. But yes, I want all of us to just take a minute and think that we have started shoving—off our own cultured language as if it's a shame to speak in Hindi. One must know English, as it is the most spoken language internationally, but please do not make the Hindi-speaking people left out of the crowd. Not following English is not a sin. One may not know it just like you may not know French or Japanese.

As Happy As A Child

IF SOMEBODY ASKS ME how would you define 'Happiness' I would like to pass on this question to my three year old daughter who can answer this far better than me. I have noticed that while we try to teach our children all about life, our children teach us what life is all about. They can teach us to be happy.

How? I would like to share this occurence. Once my 'always very keen' daughter was insisting to have water from a big pitcher to which I strictly refused assuming she'll spill the whole thing on herself. But I had to give in when she sweetly asked 'Mumma, please let me try.' And to my utter surprise she didn't tip out a single drop of water. Isn't that remarkable?

But what was even more remarkable was the beauty of her happiness which she derived from that little task. One should have seen her elation, her sense of triumph over having done it excellently. If I may be allowed to exaggerate her exhilaration could be compared to Neil Armstrong on being the first man to land on moon.

Her demeanor compelled me to ponder over my life. I begin my day running around, getting things in order, taking care of the kids, finishing my emails, and heaps of other matters only managing to complete six out of ten as per my target. And finally concluding my day, all bushed out, looking at the four things that I could not complete. That is my daily schedule.

That is true for all 'we' grown-ups. We are so busy, all our days are so eventful and our minds are so industriously engaged that we forget to be HAPPY. And to complement our already tedious monotonous life, we unlike children, wait for THE moment in life to make us feel happy which, unfortunately, will never arrive. I say this because the moment is right here; Right in your mind.

Never have I, in recent past, seen myself enjoying a small thing. When was that last time did I take time to enjoy a small scoop of icecream? When was the last time you took time to play a prank on your friend and laugh your lungs out or when did I enjoy simply doing nothing? Frank Clark, an American screenwriter said; 'Everyone is trying to accomplish something big, not realizing that life is made up of little things."

Happiness is not something which will arrive someday. It's not the time or size or price of the thing which can make us happy. It's our philosophy which gives us happiness or deprives us of any pleasure.

Actually, it's children who can rejoice little things and little moments. Like Mignon McLaughlin, The Neurotic's Notebook, 1960 said; 'Women gather together to wear silly hats, eat dainty food, and forget how unresponsive their husbands are. Men gather to talk sports, eat heavy food, and forget how demanding their wives are. Only where children gather is there any real chance of fun.'

My daughter can feel like a winner from almost anything. She can get almost as much fun out of an expensive toy as she does out of finding a small green bead from under the bed. I sincerely desire that she remains my role model for this simple and vital lesson she has taught me. And hope I do not destroy her spirit as she moves on in life as we parents feel the moral pressure to present their child as best.

"While we try to teach our children all about life,
they can teach us what life is all about"

SUCCESS

S UCCESS IS OFTEN CONFUSED to be the most profoundly intense emotion in anybody's life. When I won my first trophy, even I felt that. But then I grew up.

I am too amateur and young to enlighten anyone about this overwhelming word 'Success'. There have been innumerable quotes by world's most celebrated philosophers and legends to illustrate the same.

Even though my achievements are not as captivating as Aziz Premji, the richest man in the world or as glorious as L.N.Mittal, the richest businessman, there are a few things I have realized about success.

Success has no address, no calling cards.

Success is not a destination.

Success is not a particular moment.

Success does not make you happy.

Success is not the end of world.

My mother drew a distinction between achievement and success. She said that achievement is the knowledge that you have acquired and worked hard and done the best that is in you. Success is only an acknowledgement of it by others. I think this little piece of advice has always kept me going as I cope up with tough pressures in life.

I thank my mum for making me understand this a little too soon. Guess she sensed how the times are and how everyone is frantically a part of the 'Winning Pursuit'. Will I crack this exam? Will I get this job? Will I get a promotion, a bonus and a pay hike? Will my children do well? Will they succeed? Will I be able to fulfill my expectations? Gosh! Its intimidating!!!!!!!

Success is nice but not as important or satisfying. One should try to take pleasure in what one does. Put behind how it will turn out tomorrow or how superior is it from others. Be realistic enough to know that it is your achievement, your endeavour, your energy that brings you happiness not success.

Finish each day and be done with it. You have done what you could. Some blunders and absurdities no doubt crept in; forget them as soon as you can. Tomorrow is a new day; begin it well and serenely and with too high a spirit to be encumbered with your old nonsense.

Besides, the significance of success would diminish the day we start to understand that a lot of people who are not known to be successful also do have a life, and in fact a splendid one which they truly know how to cherish. Because they are great achievers; they have achieved the skill to work; they have attained the knowledge to learn; they have accomplished the art to be happy; they have learnt the ability to feel fulfilled. Does Success bring you all that? I have my doubts.

I Am Proud To Be An Indian

As the Independence Day arrives, I get immense pleasure to think that India is celebrating its 64 years of independence. Though, my country is still a developing nation, yet it plays an imperative role in the world economy and its diverse culture is one of its kind, found nowhere in any part of the world. So on August 15, as I stand to sing the National Anthem, paying tribute to all our freedom fighters, I raise my head up high feeling proud that I AM AN INDIAN.

But come to think of it. Are we really proud? Indianness—a tag I've noticed, most people around me resist. They like to be addressed MODS (a slang for modern). Some groups of people, who seem to dictate the rest, have adopted a style which is very much influenced by the West. Indians are known for their manners, way of communication with one another, and their friendly disposition. But in trying to imitate the west, we have forgotten few of the important components of our culture.

For instance, Conversing in Hindi is considered disdainful. Western outfits are more hip-hop these days. The other day I had worn a sari to my daughter's school and I only found people gazing at me as if I have no status or sophistication. In their language I did not belong to their society. On the contrary, I happened to meet an American on a train and she was so amazed as to how Indians tie a six-metre long cloth so beautifully and carry it with such elegance. Ironically, we look at it with such ignominy. I don't understand, why? I would not be as embarrassed for anything as I am when I see my own Indian friends mocking at someone who is less westernized.

Etiquette in terms of manners and the way of dressing differ in every country. I am not trying to say that one should not adapt or try newer styles, language or culture. The globe is shrinking & we are all getting closer to each other in many ways. My only argument is why look down upon your own ideas, customs and social behaviour? Why are people forgetting that the people abroad never ever shove off their country's values to own any other's. Unfortunately, it's we who are forgetting them and shockingly, loving to do so.

Actually no one is to be blamed in a way. Acceptance is the key. People want to be accepted well in the society. It's probably only a small segment of the populace which has developed such ideas but most of us are just blindly following it. We refuse to apply our mind into it as it's simple and satisfying to adopt acknowledged standards.

However, I refuse to follow them. I totally disagree with such notions. And, every time I observe such a thing, It not only makes me surer about my (Indian) way of life but also more resolute that I will, by all means, teach my children to respect our traditional Indian culture. Even if they adopt some western ways, they should not in the least be mortified with our own customs or conduct. They should be proud to be Indians.

The First PTM

E VER SINCE MY DAUGHTERS were born, besides their perpetually amusing growing up, I had been quite excited about one thing—When will I attend the first Parent-Teacher Meeting in school? That may sound a little strange but yes, I wished to experience the emotions when you are at the other side. Until now, PTMs had always meant an assessment of me by my guardians. I fancied knowing what it feels like to be a parent for a change.

When the day finally arrived and I returned home with her report card, I can only say that it was an overwhelming experience. I don't know why but I felt too proud to be a parent that day not because her grades were good but because I had a strong feeling sinking in. The feeling of being a mother who shall be accountable for everything my daughter does. That was quite a meticulous task that I felt blessed to have been chosen for.

It was also a realization that school is not just an institution. It is in fact an establishment where we send our child to groom up; Where we think she will get a conducive environment to grow as a sharp individual and a good human being; Where she learns to comprehend information and knowledge; Where she learns to interact with her first peer group. It can be described like a mini world where she experiences a glimpse of real one with lesser intensity.

At the PTM, you probably get a glance of the world your child has lived without you being there. I can recall how difficult it was for me to let go when Ananya and Pallavi started going to school. At the meeting, my confidence firmed up even more as I recognized that they are far more responsible than I let them be. And this filled me with pride.

Nonetheless, some of us are taking PTMs as a grade assessment platform or a place where you can gauge your child or his teachers. We overlook that a child spends only 4-6 hours in school but the remaining 70% comes from home. Thus, we must work in coordination with the teachers to bring out the best in our child and not play the blame game.

If your child is not doing as well as you desired, you need not worry. There is nothing that he or she is missing out on. It is you who is missing the broader perspective. See, if he is happy. Is he still learning without probably excelling? Is he still growing as an individual without out-shining others? Is he still exploring without being the best at extracurricular? If yes, then we must be happy. His progress can be different from our imagination but then his advancement cannot be denied.

When your child enters school and sees the cleanliness around, he is learning hygiene. When he tries to reach school on time, he is learning discipline. When he greets his teacher, he is learning etiquettes. When he shares his lunch box with his friends, he is learning socializing. When he opens his book, he is learning one part of education. When some of his classmates are not so sweet, he is learning to be tough. When he falls, he is learning to rise up high. When he allows you to go back home, he is learning to be independent.

So next time when you enter the school premises, you must thank every little process that took place here to teach your child so much instead of just looking at a 4 page report card which only talks about one little aspect of your child.

People ask me what I want my child to be. I had various thoughts before. I was unsure and worried about how the school takes care of my child. Whether their academics are good enough and are they sufficiently paying attention to ECA? All my doubts stand addressed and now I tell them that I just want them to be HAPPY always—as happy as their childhood.

"My Promise to my children

I am your Mother. I will stalk you,

flip out on you, lecture you, drive you insane, be your worst nightmare

and hunt you down like a bloodhound when needed

because I LOVE YOU!

When you understand that, I will

know you are a responsible adult. You will

NEVER find someone who loves, prays, cares

and worries about you more than I do!"

Listen Earnestly

"**I** KNOW THAT YOU BELIEVE you understand what you think I said, but I'm not sure you realize that what you heard is not what I meant."

Is that bewildering? Go through it one more time and imagine your kid saying it to you. I have sensed that we as adults do not give a very patient hearing to our children—be it their problems; their queries; their fears. We tend to take it for granted that they do not know as much as we do and we understand them much more than they themselves. And that's where the error begins.

We love to laugh at their humorous conversations. We cherish how they cuddle us. We feel proud at their discoveries. We worry how well they are performing. But when it comes to giving our dedicated time to them, either we have scores of tasks waiting to be finished before that or the fatigue takes a toll on us. We fail to listen to them unwearyingly.

Once, at my friend's place, Aryan, her son was trying to have a word with her mum for last 15 minutes. First a call and then a doorbell and afterwards some tit-bit household errand, almost tried his patience. Like a curious youngster, he became obstinate about asking one question only to hear back a holler from his mother. 'Will you please keep quiet? I am doing something which is totally unavoidable.' He felt quite disturbed.

I figured out that he only wanted to ask if he can use his mom's pen to complete his drawing.

Reason it out. How much time would that have taken had she allowed him to speak; A second or a two, Certainly not longer. That really pinched me. I felt bad for him and more because there came a slight guilty feeling that unconsciously I may have done the same to my children. When Pallavi would start narrating the whole day's experience at school, I would interrupt 'Did you finish your food?' and I would obviously hear a no. And then, 'why did you not eat?' "What did the teacher teach you today?' "Did you get homework?' and so on.

I happened to completely ignore what she was wanting to talk about. We always tend to take them for granted and make them wait because we are so obsessed with our priorities which are far more important than their questions which are so obvious.

There's another thing that came to my mind. Whenever they come up with any fear like being afraid of a dog or darkness or sometimes my daughter would say I am afraid I will fall off the steps. I would laugh them off. How stupid? How can you be afraid of the dog? They don't do anything. Darkness does no harm. It's the same house and sleeping with lights on is such a silly idea. Why would you fall off the steps suddenly? You walk carefully and nothing happens.

Wow! how comforting was that? It's like when I am in tears and my friend not only mocks at me for crying but also refuses to acknowledge that a problem even exists. That can be so annoying. Obviously, I feel only worse and decide never to go back to this friend who instead of listening to me only made me feel ridiculed.

The better way to handle my daughter's fears would have been to just listen to her:

There is a tiger in my room,' said Pallavi

'Did he bite you?, said me

'No,' said she

'Did he scratch you?'

'No,'

'Then he is a friendly tiger,' 'He will not hurt you. Go back to sleep."
And that's it.

Mind you those issues may seem beside the point or fears may seem irrelevant to us but for them they are real. Even though their problems are so petty according to us, they are all genuine which need to be addressed as soon as possible and in fact more urgently than ours. And let me tell you that children have never been very good at listening to their elders, but they have never failed to imitate them. So if you take note of their words, so will they.

Listen earnestly to anything your children want to tell you, no matter what. IF you do not listen earnestly to the little stuff when they are little, they won't tell you the big stuff when they are big. Because to them all of it has always been big.

WHAT IS PRECIOUS?

WHAT IS PRECIOUS? LET me think. Hmmmm . . . . Diamonds, sapphires? Or from my sister's mouth, it could be her ATM? My darling daughter has a different answer though. Kids are so creative and fundamental that they sometimes end up teaching us the more valuable lessons that we tend to forget as we get on with our busy hard erring lives.

Sometime ago, I was travelling with my daughters in a train. In some way they always look forward to a train journey much more than any other. The mention of it brings in the fervor in them, to gear up for the expedition. Mind it, it does sound like an expedition and nothing less. It means lots of munching, surplus play time and of course unremitting attention from us. And like each time they were all set with their whole assortment of colours, drawing books, stationery, story book, clay etc. for a mere 4 hour journey.

They particularly prefer the 'red' train (Rajdhani) to the blue one (Shatabdi); the reason being the super attractive upper berth to play on. Suhaani insisted to climb on to play with her sisters. While I rose to push her up, her dismayed look to see her crayons fall off her lap, was quite a sight. And like as if the most meticulous girl, instantly and painstakingly she picked them up all and caressed them to carefully handover to me.

I was only left wondering if those were her most prizest possession and contemplating in astonishment as what exactly precious was I carrying in my handbag.

I only felt amused at her diligent and insufferably precious performance. I was happy. One coz she was learning to take care of her things on her own and valuing the littlest and most inexpensive things too. But more so coz I learnt to appreciate what precious really is. Not my money, house or jewellery but the real riches that lie deep within your soul and that can never be taken away.

I think its incredible to observe how she collects her little toys, her clips and a few other knick-knacks each day and arrange them like there is nothing more dear in this world. She will find so much fun in exploring her new toy taking pleasure in the entire discovery. What I feel is that this art that children have is remarkable.

I am sure this is the fairer truth of life what my doll is chasing day in day out and not what we adults are. We consider gold and jade to be precious treasures, but we let pass the little things which bring us true happiness.

At this point I cannot resist to mention what happened last week. While I was away to my friends place, Suhaani my new teacher, who persuaded to stay at my aunt's place for that time, went missing without anybody's knowledge. I panicked and rushed back to find her. I was in the gush of emotions of so many 'what ifs?.' What if she is picked up by someone? What is she is hurt by a car? Within a span of one minute I can't imagine the things my mind visualized. Next I broke down wondering how I would do without her. I know I was over reacting but found it impossible to hold.

Unexpectedly, I get a call from home saying that she has reached back home on her own. God bless. Wow! She is just three and did she really walk back a kilometer to reach home safely? I was angry at her, relieved for she was safe and honestly a little proud that she knew how to take care of herself.

Even though I had decided that I won't talk to her when I reach back to make her realize how inappropriate her action was, nevertheless I hugged her too tight not letting her go for almost an hour. I certainly understood how invaluable she meant to me; probably much more than anything else in this world.

And then I knew who to thank for all the little miracles in our lives.—the precious shield of God that guards us well in all the darkest valleys that we must traverse.

"Life becomes **precious** and more special to us when we look for the little everyday miracles and get excited about the privileges of simply being human"

A HUG IS ALL I NEED . . . .

OVER THE YEARS OF rearing my little ones, I realized that they are no more new born tiny tots whom I can fuss over. They are young individuals already at the age of four. They understand, react, feel and go through the same set of emotions that we do; only in a bit more animated way. My daughter Ananya helped me recognize that while I try to instill the right values in her, it doesn't necessarily mean that she will do that right away and it is as simple for her as I tell her. She needs a little time like we all do when handling a new situation. So this come straight from her heart through my words.

> After you drop me to school
> I might miss you, I start to weep
> School is essential;
> I also intend to Agree
> But I despise all your preachings that precede
> I feel sad and sometimes a hug is all I need

Once I lie to you
Coz I am afraid to tell you my deed
It is unruly behaviour
I understand what you teach
But I don't like you scolding, I do not pay heed
I feel sad and sometimes a hug is all I need

As I put across numerous inquests
About nature, people, cars and speed
I know I am peculiarly curious
Your staying power exceeds
But I am gloomy to see my contentment unachieved
I feel sad and sometimes a hug is all I need

While I play to the core of my heart
And you put me to sleep
Only coz going to school is a must
You explain me to deep
But I dislike your discipline supersedes
I feel sad and sometimes a hug is all I need

When you refuse to get me my favourite toy
Because of my mischief
I realize my mistake
Time after time, I go to extremes
But my apologies do not make you pleased
I feel sad and sometimes a hug is all I need

When I behave like a nag
Refusing to eat my meals
It is not about the taste;
I just hate force feed
Still I push myself only so that you feel relieved
I feel sad and sometimes a hug is all I need

Mommy! Did I ever tell you
I may be stubborn and hard to concede
Juvenile but sharp, I plead
Don't make your suggestion as if a court's decreed
Coz I also feel like you all feel.
As I grow up into an individual indeed
Sometimes, A hug is all I need.

Re-assurance, Yet Again

THIS MORNING MY FRIEND called up. She was very perturbed about the disorderliness of the school. Actually nothing major but because of their upcoming primary event, none of us are informed in good time about the latest developments and even though we are getting used to the last minute thingy but we obviously dislike it. We suddenly become incredibly doubtful of the once most wanted institution chosen by us for a secure beginning of our little one.

Candidly, I was also a little unhappy when my five year old told me yesterday that she could not have lunch as they had no time amidst the whole rehearsal going on for their cultural evening. So here it goes. Both of us found a good opportunity to expel all the suppressed anger about the mismanagement. But you know if I look back, I would own up that it was me who was upset that Ananya was hungry all through the day. She wasn't. In fact she was singing her own praises about the hardwork she was putting to her practice and which is why couldn't manage to eat. My mind read that but my heart decided to overlook that.

I have faith that she is learning many new-fangled things and becoming confident to conduct herself before smaller challenges but then comes a protective 'Me' in between; who wants to keep assuring her own self that I am taking care of my kid in the best possible way.

There is one more moment where I struggle through the same sentiments. Even though as parents we have always decided that our children will never ever be compelled to outshine their peers academically or otherwise. All the same I will admit that a tiny thought does flash through my mind if sometimes Pallavi is not given a role to play in her class performance or Suhaani's beautiful project is not appreciated or Ananya, despite our regular home-revisions is not recognized as the best in class. Actually, it's a human psychology. We do not mind their not doing extremely well but when we see somebody else being distinguished and applauded; we do get a self doubt. We question.

Not all the times but a very few times, you do ponder if you can do something better for your child or are you missing out on any effort on your part? And here you are. You need assurance again. I have been quite fortunate to have made a very good friend, Harinder. We mutually sort out and assure each other. And thankfully, she never exaggerates anything. But I have noticed a few parents making a fuss over it.

I have started to put into practice a couple of ideas now. One, I always remind myself that what my daughter achieves in day—to—day school activities is not THE ONLY thing which will lead to her successful life. It will be the positive attitude, right conviction and immense exposure which will evolve her into a confident person. This alone cannot come from school and has no linkage to her being crowned the best in class. It will come from what 'I' do because as I understand, of all the people in the world, she is observing me the most and absorbing so many things that I don't even notice about myself. So, I better be up to it and set a fine example rather than confuse her with my bamboozling expectations.

Second, it is absolutely acceptable if she does not have any extra-ordinary achievements but remains a warm and bright individual. I have seen my comrades doing some amazing stuffs and earning a grand living for themselves despite their poor school records. So, I better be taking it easy.

As a next step, when Pallavi tells me that Suhaani did not perform well at her Bal-Sabha (special assembly), I do not worry. I only glance at the smile Suhaani carries since she is very happy and satisfied for the fact that she was a part of that performance irrespective of how well it went. That is what is really important and I have learnt to hold myself then and not spoil that ecstasy in their heart.

Teaching Them To Say Bye

I HAVE SEEN MY FRIENDS telling me stories of how they would silently abscond from their house as they left their child with the grandparents to sneak out for a movie. Why I use the word 'abscond' is precisely how they describe it to me? Leaving their child back home is made to sound like such a big deal.

I differ from their thoughts. I think it is nasty of us to do that. Look at it from a child's point of view. They hate to let us go because they do not imagine a world without us. They have solely depended upon us since their birth. And suddenly not finding their parents around, without even a faint idea is like heart-breaking. Imagine how you would feel if you do not find your spouse in the house when you wake up in the morning. You feel a little odd. Don't you? And mind it, your child feels shattered if you do that to her.

I am not saying, don't step out. I am just saying that choose a more appropriate way to go about it. Over these years, through my experience, I suggest that we should always tell them and go, even if that amounts to a little crying at that point of time. If you are afraid that they will be quite upset, you should start preparing them a few hours in advance. Initially, it does invite a lot of melodrama I admit, but then it starts to work. Slipping out of the house without making them aware will only mean more complaints.

When I get ready to go out anywhere, anxiously Ananya asks me "Mom! Where are you going? Why are you not staying with us?"

Instantly, I ask her only one question "do you want me to really tell you the truth or lie to you?

"No, Mumma! I am a big girl now; you tell me only the truth."

So I explain it to her that I have to go now for a little while and will be back soon to play with her. And she bids a sweet smiling goodbye, thereby making it easier for herself and lightening for me. I definitely feel less guilty when she willingly sends me.

Quite honestly, this change has not been the result of any overnight maturity. I used to tell her even when she was only a few months old. Obviously, she could not respond much then but I believed that she was so connected to me that she has a right to know. When she was grown up enough to sense that I am leaving, she would get cranky or cry. And now she has matured to handle this very well. I am so proud to see her so responsible. Not telling her always seemed simple but my conscience never allowed knowing that she would certainly search for me restlessly. Teaching her to say Goodbye was less complicated I guess.

BEDTIME, THE BEST TIME

MY SISTER IS ALWAYS very curious to know as to how am I so aware about our mythology and traditions. I would attribute this bit of knowledge and understanding to my grandfather and my parents who passed on such small pieces of facts in the form of short stories. I still have faint glimpses in my mind about how I used to relish those tales.

I see the same enthusiasm in my kids as they prepare themselves for sleep, crawl into their beds and wait for me to read a book as they fall asleep. The classic fairytale stories, imaginative books with cartoon drawings are piled high next to their bed waiting to be read each night.

They say that the best writers are always good readers first. I am sure there are many more benefits that children derive from reading as research would put it. But I really look forward to this time of the day as it is also about spending time together and growing together with my children. I know it gives them language and imagination much more than any school can give.

I also came to appreciate its importance after a very long time. Every day the three of them would most excitedly sit across with one book each, which frankly it was irrelevant to check if I was free or interested to read. I had to, period.

I remember Ananya came crying from school one day. She was not assigned any role in a play her class was preparing for which she was desperate. I totally related to her feelings but did not know how to handle it of course as she was too young to be able to rationalize. So I narrated this brief story.

As children bring their broken toys
with tears for us to mend,
I brought my broken dreams to God,
because He was my friend.
But then, instead of leaving Him,
in peace, to work alone;
I hung around and tried to help,
with ways that were my own.
At last, I snatched them back and cried,
"How can you be so slow?"
"My child," He said,
"What could I do?
You never did let go."

I told her to just share her problem with God and sleep without any worries and comforted her that she would feel much better the next day. For the sincere girl she is, she did in fact leave it to Him. And next day the thrill on her face, when she entered home after school, was worth a click. She was breathlessly happy to tell me that God really did help her. Somehow her class teacher had changed her mind and gave her a character to play.

It was that simple? Was it? When I recited that story I truly did not know, it was going to leave that much of an impression on her. But yes, that made me realize what story time does. Lack of time and stress prevents most of us from being able to read to our children each night. But these ten minutes of your day, I assure will bring lots more than just a routine exercise. It will be gratifying to know that tales that you are sharing will craft in them an emotional life lesson that will be subconsciously instilled in your child.

Remember the time when you snuggled with your child with the scent of baby powder under your nose? We think such moments are gone ever since our snuggler has started to go to school. It hasn't. Next time save time and read out to her and you can help her become an even better individual than what she is right now.

LEARNING TO SHARE

AMUSINGLY, SUHAANI LIKE A few other kids I am sure, loves to keep me to her only. She is very possessive about her belongings including 'me'. Her feelings are genuine I am convinced but when she turns into a little monster over this thing, I must say, I feel confused, spoilt and pleased at the same time. Her exaggerated emotions pushed me to put this down so vividly.

I got my new toy today, I exclaim
A new teddy bear and a plane
It's not a big deal, to my sis I feign
But I adore you for this game
To my mom who bears the sweetest name
And adds warmth to the same

As I go to school, I put it on the window pane
No one dare touch it; so intact it remains
All of you must share, mommy ingrains
I relinquish gloomily without any restrain
To my mom who bears the sweetest name
And adds warmth to the same

Though, I must put forth my complaint
This ordeal seems unconstrained
We have mutual clothes, dolls and trains
I should get hers but giving away sounds insane
But I still do it for the sake of a fair game,
To my mom who bears the sweetest name
And adds warmth to the same

I keep quiet and abstain
My liberal thinking and patience all in vain
When you ask me to share your time and embrace
I can impart with anything but on this, I constrain
"Am I not your choicest bear?" please proclaim
To my mom who bears the sweetest name
And adds warmth to the same

It's About Time

RECENTLY I WATCHED AN amazing movie. It was beautifully filmed and unabashedly sincere. The gentleman in the movie can travel in time. So, he decides to make his world a better place which doesn't turn out as easy as it might appear to us. His unique gift couldn't save him from the sorrows and ups and downs that affect all families, everywhere. There are great limits to what time travel can achieve which cannot solve all your problems.

There are so many days; even I feel, wish I had a magic wand which helped me rectify so many deeds of mine. All of us do. Oh! How I wish I had not answered him like that? Or why did I yell at such and such person? Or what could I have done to make it nicer for somebody? All these thoughts keep crossing our minds.

I had a strange dream last night. I dreamt that I was extremely late to drive the kids to school; Missed my ever-essential walk; couldn't reach for an urgent meeting; And there I was, all tense picking back the three of them; only to know that Pallavi has had a bad day too. To add more to it, ever—clingy Suhaani has chosen to try my patience even more today—A perfect description of a crazy day. I woke up very heavy that morning.

Why I call this dream strange is not because it had something very unusual about my day. I can be behind schedule some days and of course

Pallavi can have an unexciting day as well. What was bizarre was that I seemed to be re-living my dream. That's exactly how things were taking place.

When I looked at the clock, I chose not to panic. I just hugged my kiddies letting them know that it's not the end of the world to be late for school. We did in fact manage it well in time along with a little adventure and fun. Furthermore, I felt so rejuvenated to have laughed with them that walk was the last thing on my mind. I returned home and after finishing my meeting, reached school. On seeing Pallavi in a cranky mood, instead of questioning her like a protective mom, I only embraced her while she sat in my lap and told her how she made my day's start so amusing today. Instantly, which only children can ever manage, she swapped her mood to a smiling happy one. Since all was good, Suhaani's clinging on did not make it difficult either.

And here I was at the end of a perfect day because I cherished every bit of it. I wish life was as simple as I have put it in the paragraphs above and we were as prepared for any crisis any day. But that cannot be the case always. Even though, these instances are nowhere near to the difficulties that we can face but if we make this philosophy as the way of life, things would be more pleasurable.

This little dream was certainly God sent. He wanted to remind me something—Remind me that it's about time now that I start living each moment thoroughly as though this day is the full and final one of its kind and discover the truth, that in the end, making the most of life may not need time travel at all. Perfect moments never arrive. You fish out the perfection from each one of them.

Love Unconditional

MY FAMILY OFTEN ASKS me why I love Suhaani so much more than others. No, in all sincerity, its certainly not like that. I adore all three of them utterly. However, I find it irresistible to mention that Suhaani's affection towards me is absolute. She treats me like a princess who deserves an enhanced adoration. It is hilarious how she used to be green with her dad for even sharing popcorn from my plate.

Although my eldest one Ananya is just perfect to be my best friend as she is so mature and concerned about my happiness already. And her twin sister Pallavi is such a delicate darling whose gorgeous looking eyes and strong will inspires me to look up to her. But there is something about Suhaani that is distinctive. If truth be told, she is the most mischievous and gets my scolding nearly all the time.

However, what is special about her is that she loves me UNCONDITIONALLY. She has made me experience the relevance of that expression. I don't think I have ever loved anyone like that. No matter how much I yell at her, she will still rush and hug me wanting a promise each time that 'I am nobody else's but her mom'. I mean it is crazy. She has never got angry at me despite the fact that I get rude, busy and sometimes so pre-occupied. She can wait for me incessantly until I kiss her goodnight.

I think her name befits her character. She is most cheerful and caring and her company as charming. She accepts me the way I am. Now that is categorical. I have a thing about the way she makes me sleep on her soft and supple palm and give me a tight hug when I put her to bed. Though I barely fit into them but it is totally divine.

And any day I am a little low, I know where to go. I just hold her close. And by the look of my eyes she knows I am not fine. She will get water for me and embrace me until I leave her. I can't explain you Suhaani what it means to me. All I know is that not many get what I have. And I cannot thank you enough for these gestures. The three of you are the bestest gift from God to me.

I also know that once you grow up, this might change because you will learn the rules of this world. You will learn what's fair and what's not and you will learn to reason it out. You will not come running to me like now, even when I get upset with you. I very well understand that. I assure that it's going to be absolutely fine. I want you to grow up smart of course. What I am precisely scared of is getting used to the unconditional love that you shower upon me. And then I won't know where to go.

For this reason, I don't want to let go any moment presently with you as no matter how badly I perform in any domain of life; be it the house or work or upbringing all three of you, in your eyes I know I will always be a super hero.

THE LITTLE PALLAVI THAT CAN

I WAS READING OUT THIS interesting story to them last night. In the tale, a long train must be pulled over a high mountain. Larger engines are asked to pull the train; for various reasons they refuse. The request is sent to a small engine, who agrees to try. The engine succeeds in pulling the train over the mountain while repeating its motto: "I-think-I-can".

The story of the little engine has been told and retold many times. The underlying theme is the same—a stranded train is unable to find an engine willing to take it on over difficult terrain to its destination. Only the little blue engine is willing to try and, while repeating the mantra, overcomes a seemingly impossible task.

This little story has depicted this dogma very well in such a crisp simple way. And while I read it, I evidently related it to Pallavi a lot. By the very first look, she looks like a sweet dainty girl. She is an attractive soul with an ever smiling face and a very melodious voice.

As her mother, even though she is so young, I would say perseverance is the greatest attribute she possesses. Inherently though she is a little laid back a few times but if she decides to do a certain thing, I have seen her following it to the end. I have seen this in little things in her day to day life. When it comes to doing her homework, one should notice the excitement in her eyes. She never does it with a burden. She has the charm to learn new things, interact with newer people and of course enjoy what she does.

Amusingly, just like the little train she believes in her self-created mantra 'abra-ka-dabra' which she picked up at one of the magic shows. She has the confidence and trust that when she says so, be it anything on earth, it does come true; the most favourite time being her way back from school. It works on the traffic to move faster she assumes. And sometimes we also have a little fun seeking her opinion light-heartedly, as to whether our decision on some issues will turn to our favour or no. If I may be permitted to say the truth, as a mother I have the faith that it does.

I can say that Ananya is intelligent, Suhaani is strong but Pallavi is a willful girl. And I know that with this attitude, she is bound to go far ahead in life. No wonder I call her a lots of names, my butterfly, pavu, dolly, shona but my favourite one—which I shall always tell her when she grows up is "P for Pallavi and P for Perseverance."

When she is an adult I will remind her of this aspect always and preach her that there are very many people who shall tell you that you can't but what you've got to do is turn around and say 'Watch me'.

UNPARALLELED

O NCE THERE WERE TWO sisters who were great friends and always played together. However, one day they had a huge argument about one of their toys. In the end, they decided that from then on they would only be allowed to play with their own individual toys.

They had so many of them that they agreed to spend the next day sorting out which toy belonged to whom. So the next day each sister got to work, making a pile of her own things. When they had finished doing the big toys it was time to sort the little stuff. However, they had already taken so long that it was time for bed, so they left the small toys for the next day. In the end, seeing the accumulated mountains of stuff they had divided, one of them decided to call the fight off and gave away all her toys to the other one.

What a wonderful deliberation? Due to one prudent action, they were merrily playing together again, picking everything up, careless of whether they were mixing it all. They looked really happy, enjoying themselves to the maximum.

If you are wondering whose story is that? It is in fact Ananya who realized how foolish they had been and it would be no fun without Pallavi and Suhaani. It would be too monotonous alone and she would derive no pleasure like that.

Out rightly, she has been the most sensible girl I have. Not once but each day I have seen her assume the act of responsibility to pacify the fights between them without my help. She will cheer up her sisters in case they are having a bad day; help me in my daily chores; compliment me just to make me smile; and remember all instructions that I give them for the day. What is significantly unexpected is the way she defends Suhaani and Pallavi when I scold any one of them requesting me to give her just five minutes until she gets them to some reconciliation.

I think one cannot all of a sudden, create it. One is born with such traits or else I refuse to believe that such a small girl begins to have a cool, calm and collected behavior without my consciously explaining it to her.

I am only rendered speechless to notice how playfully she encourages Suhaani to do the writing work which I certainly couldn't have done her way. Then she does not appear to be only two years older to her. She seems like her 'chotu maa'(young mommy) which Suhaani indeed addresses her at times teasingly.

My dear Ananya, when you were born, 'Ananya' meaning the unparalleled seemed just the apt name for you. I understand the reason better now. You really are so unique and bring such enticing moments to all of us which we can't help but treasure. Your vivid simplicity is articulation in the most beautiful form. Always cherish it.

AFTERWORD

WHEN I TRY TO remember my childhood days, I know that I was more relaxed and fun-filled only because I was so unaware of life's demanding confrontations. And when I look at my children, I feel the urge to re-adopt that carefree attitude because I have understood the secret of happiness in life. The most blissful people are not the ones who HAVE the best of everything. They are the ones who MAKE the best of everything. And who knows that art better than the children.

This book is a treasure I created for myself and to bring a sweet reminiscence to all three of them later. And I will say that even though raising children is a task so meticulous and demanding, we must realize there is nothing more precious than this.